CONFRONTING AMERICA'S MORAL CRISIS

BOOKS BY THOMAS HAUSER

Non-Fiction

Missing
The Trial of Patrolman Thomas Shea
For Our Children
    (with Frank Macchiarola)
The Family Legal Companion
The Black Lights: Inside the World of
    Professional Boxing
Final Warning: The Legacy of Chernobyl
Muhammad Ali: His Life and Times
Muhammad Ali: Memories
Arnold Palmer: A Personal Journey
Confronting America's Moral Crisis
    (with Frank Macchiarola)

Fiction

Ashworth & Palmer
Agatha's Friends
The Beethoven Conspiracy
Hanneman's War
The Fantasy
Dear Hannah
The Hawthorne Group

TITLE: Confronting America's Moral
Crisis

AUTHOR: Tom Hauser
Frank Macchiarola

PRICE: $6.95

PUBLICATION DATE: Sept. 11, 1995

CONFRONTING AMERICA'S MORAL CRISIS

THOMAS HAUSER AND
FRANK MACCHIAROLA

HASTINGS HOUSE *Book Publishers*
Mamaroneck • New York

Library of Congress Catalog Card Number 95-056056
ISBN 0-8038-9376-0

Text design by Elizabeth Woll

Printed in the United States of America

10 9 8 7 6 5 4 3 2 1

MORAL GROWTH begins in childhood. We dedicate this book to some wonderful children whom we have watched grow since their birth. The greatest gift we could wish for them is that they continue to experience the joy and fulfillment that come with living a principled life:

Cathy and Jessica Hauser
Billy, Lisa, and Keith Hoffmann
Joseph, Michael, and Frank Macchiarola
David and Kara Sloman

ACKNOWLEDGMENTS

During the course of writing this book, we exchanged ideas with many people. We're particularly indebted to the following individuals who shared their thoughts with us in a formal interview setting: Richard Bellman, Lonny Block, Rev. Calvin Butts, Ramsey Clark, Karen Dressner, Yvonne Fink, John Gardner, Alan Gartner, Joel Hirschtritt, Tom Hoover, Jerry Izenberg, Cheryl Koopman, Jeffrey Morris, Wali Muhammad, Arlene Pedone, Walter Stafford, Lewis Steel, Margaret Steinfels, David Steinmann, Most Rev. Joseph M. Sullivan.

CONTENTS

1

THE REASONS FOR THIS BOOK

M ORALS ARE at the heart of how people relate to one another. They reflect what we think of ourselves.

There are many people in the United States who have good values and live highly principled, ethical lives. But in recent years, it has become painfully clear that moral values in this country aren't what they ought to be. In some respects, they might be improving. But overall, they are eroding, and have been for much of our lifetime.

In and of itself, this erosion is hardly a new phenomenon. The history of the United States is one of moral cycles. Indeed, at the end of the "Roaring Twenties"—a decade similar in many respects to the 1980s—Walter Lippmann wrote, "The wisdom deposited in our moral ideals is heavily obscured at the present time. We continue to use the language of morality, having no other which we can use. But the words are so hackneyed that their meanings are concealed, and it is very hard, especially for young people, to realize that virtue is really good and relevant. Morality has become so stereotyped, so thin and verbal, so encrusted with pious fraud, that our generation has almost forgotten that virtue was not invented in Sunday schools but derives originally from a profound realization of the character of human life."

Lippmann's words were prescient of today's world. In fact, if there has been a change in the past two-thirds of a century, it is that moral values have further decayed. Our society is plagued by corruption and disorder. Too many Americans ignore matters of right and wrong. They are interested only in self-serving results, and rationalize away unethical conduct. Cheating and lying are accepted as common. There's a moral black hole in many lives. And if some people find a way to skirt moral values or live by them conveniently, others seem to have no morals at all.

The United States likes to think of itself as a nation that values and cares for its children. But the truth is, we don't. There are too many instances when we don't feed children properly or educate them adequately, both of which are moral imperatives. Child abuse is horrifyingly prevalent and on the rise. Oftentimes, life itself doesn't seem to matter. We read regularly of twelve-year-old girls throwing their own newborn infants down incinerator shafts or into garbage cans. We read on, and learn that the same twelve-year-old's guardian was oblivious to the fact that she was pregnant at all. Meanwhile, doctors debate "medical ethics" in terms of genetic engineering, fetal tissue research, organ transplants, and a patient's right to die. Their dialogue avoids the fact that quality health care simply is not available for many American families with children, and that 37 million Americans have no health insurance at all.

Personal safety is as much a moral issue as the right to decent health care and a quality education. Yet, there are places in this country, most notably in our inner cities, where Americans no longer enjoy what should be the fundamental expectation that their lives will be free from violence. There's a "crime of the month" in many urban areas— "wilding," ritual assaults, young men killed for leather jackets. More Americans are murdered on the streets of our country in fifty-five hours than died in combat in the entire Persian Gulf War. There are twice as many people living homeless or addicted to crack in the United States than were subjugated to the tyranny of Saddam Hussein in Kuwait.

Moral failings among many of America's "have-nots" are explained by some on the theory that people with little stake in a system have no reason for concern regarding that system's corruption and fall. But such logic ignores the stark reality that America's moral dilemma cuts across class lines. Some of the worst moral offenders in this country have the most to gain from "the system" being preserved. Ethical considerations are viewed as obstacles by many of America's business elite. Oftentimes, in a corporate environment, it takes courage to raise ethical issues at all. The inner-city crime of the moment has its counterpart in a deluge of white-collar crime. Defense contractors systematically overcharge on an array of complex weapons systems. Banks launder illegal drug money in violation of federal banking laws. Brokerage houses engage in check kiting, insider trading, and illegal practices at Treasury auctions. Adulterated apple juice intended for infant use is intentionally mislabeled "pure."

Government misconduct seems to have spiralled out of control. We learned that the Department of Housing and Urban Development was mired in scandal, and that the cost to the public to remedy the situation would be $4 billion to $8 billion. That's a staggering number; hard to grasp. But then we learned that $8 billion was very small compared with the cost of delinquency at our savings and loan institutions—an industry supposedly closely regulated by federal and state monitors. Irresponsible, and in some cases criminal, bankers made investments and lent huge sums of money to entrepreneurs of dubious character. The deals were supervised by lawyers and sanctioned by accountants from some of America's finest firms. The S&L deposits were protected by government-backed insurance. And now $500 billion is gone.

How much is $500 billion? Roughly $2,000 for every American man, woman, and child. Or calculated differently: if someone took a stack of $100 bills and laid them end to end, $500 billion would stretch to the moon and back. It would circle the earth at the equator nineteen times.

Even the manner in which leaders ask for our votes has changed. In 1960, accepting the Democratic party's nomination for the presidency, John F. Kennedy declared, "The New Frontier of which I speak is not a set of promises; it is a set of challenges. It sums up, not what I intend to offer the American people, but what I intend to ask of them." And in the same spirit, on the day he was inaugurated, Kennedy urged each and every American to "Ask not what your country can do for you. Ask what you can do for your country."

Kennedy's words moved a nation and inspired much of what was good in the 1960s. Yet, twenty years later, the pendulum had swung, and in 1980, Ronald Reagan ushered in a new era. The issue Reagan put before every American in his climactic debate with Jimmy Carter was "Are *you* better off than you were four years ago?" Self-interest had replaced sacrifice and community values. And many of America's problems have burgeoned out of control since then. Now we're well into yet another administration. The Reagan-Bush years are over. But they were terminated, not as the result of a commitment to moral excellence by the electorate, but largely because of personalized economic concerns. And if the 1994 election returns are an accurate indicator, self-interest remains far ahead of community values on the list of America's electoral priorities.

Morals are more than abstract principles.

Indeed, moral values have always been at the core of America's public philosophy and national goals. But, now, too many of us at all levels of society have opted out of trying to make our communities better, and we pursue primarily selfish ends. This self-indulgence hasn't made Americans happier. Rather, the contrary appears to be true. But what the unchecked pursuit of self-interest has done is endanger our sense of national purpose. Americans are no longer united on the great goals that we as a society must achieve. Our ability to finance much-needed change has been drained by multi-billion-dollar losses. Both in the way we address major political problems and the manner in which we treat each other as individuals, we need to rethink fundamental moral questions and respond with action. We must face up to what America as a nation has become, and then do something about it.

The United States is a great country. For more than two centuries, it has inspired the world, serving as a beacon of idealism and hope. It has survived many eras in which "the world didn't seem to work"—depressions, wars, trials of many kinds. But America isn't as old and enduring as we might think it to be. A child born on July 4, 1776, could easily have lived to be eighty years old. On the day of that child's death—July 4, 1856—another child might have been born. And were that second child to have lived eighty years, its death would have occurred on July 4, 1936; a mere fifty-nine years ago.

In other words, our nation has been in existence for less than three lifetimes. And it stands now at a point where its people must choose between self-indulgence and the finest of American ideals. We believe that one path will lead to a flourishing America. But if the other road is taken, the American Century may well be succeeded by a century of ethical obsolescence and mediocrity.

For some time, as the authors of this book, we have been talking with people whose lives represent a commitment to moral excellence. A few of them are famous; most are not. Some grew up in stable families; others come from broken homes. Some are religious; others have thought very little about God. But the people we have sought out share the view that each person is an architect of society; that when individuals know the difference between right and wrong and choose to do what is right, they and society are strengthened.

We have drawn on the insights of these men and women and added our own. Our assumption is that there are problems with moral values in America; that there are problems in defining them, putting them in a value-oriented framework, communicating them, translating them into public policy, and living with them in a way that doesn't cause resentment or anger among others. And we have been looking for ways to talk with people about the state of our society and how it can be improved.

This book is part of that process. It's not meant to be all encompassing. It's not a lengthy philosophical tome. Rather, it's designed to promote discussion and thought, and give people some practical insight into how to fulfill their responsibilities to society and each other. We don't expect you, the reader, to agree with everything we have to say. By definition, many people won't. But we hope that, after reading this book, you will think a little more often about moral values and what you and others can do to make our country a better place to live. We hope that you will discuss the issues we raise with your parents, children, mentors, and friends. And we believe that, in the end, you will share our conclusion that moral values must ultimately relate to a broad definition of the public good.

2

WHAT ARE MORAL VALUES ALL ABOUT?

WHERE DO THEY COME FROM?

WHY ARE THEY IMPORTANT?

FOR THOSE who believe in a literal interpretation of the Bible, the Qur'an, or other sacred texts, moral values are the product of Divine command. God created Adam and Eve; His will has been made known on Earth through a series of prophets and other messengers; and the degree to which each of us follows God's law will determine whether we are granted salvation or condemned to eternal damnation.

But, obviously, there are divergent views on the origin and evolution of humankind. Some of these views presuppose the existence of God, while others don't. Some see early humans as gentle and benign, while others characterize them as savage, selfish, and ignorant. Inevitably, though, at some juncture, these competing beliefs coincide. For, as Bertrand Russell has written, "Apart from the question of whether man is really so glorious as the theologians of evolution say he is, life on this planet is almost certainly temporary. The earth will grow cold, or the atmosphere will fly off, or there will be an insufficiency of water, or the sun will burst, and the human race will ultimately die out. Such an event is of little importance from the point of view of orthodox theology, since men are immortal and will continue to exist in heaven and hell when none are left on earth. But the importance of man, which is the one indispensable dogma of theologians, receives no support from a scientific view of the future of the solar system. Do we survive death in any sense, and if so, do we survive for a time or forever? Has the universe a purpose, or is it mere chaos and jumble in which the natural laws that we think we find are only a fantasy generated by our own love of order? Has life more importance in it than astronomy would lead us to suppose, or is our emphasis upon life mere parochialism and self-importance? I do not know the answer to these questions, and I do not believe that anybody else does, but I think human life would be impoverished if they were forgotten or if definite answers were accepted without adequate evidence. To keep alive the interest in such questions and to scrutinize suggested answers is one of the functions of philosophy."

It was Socrates who began the formal search for moral definitions in rational philosophical thought. Most of what is known of his teachings has been preserved in Plato's dialogues. Aristotle, born fifteen years after the death of Socrates, studied with Plato for two decades, and built upon the work of his predecessors, positing that while mathematics and theology lend themselves to exact infallible knowledge, moral theory offers only probable and approximate conclusions.

The next great wave of change in Western moral thought evolved with Christianity during the Dark Ages and medieval times. Then, in the early sixteenth century, the growth of competing Christian denominations, science, and the rise of nation-states led to the study of "modern ethics." Morality was still seen as a discipline to prepare men and women for heaven. But its foundation was broadened to include the components of reason, sentiment, utility, and virtue. And it was understood that morality served two very important secular purposes.

The first of these purposes relates directly to the survival of society. If each person lived on a little island, we could give in to every impulse we feel and affect no one but ourselves. But none of us is isolated in that manner. Everyone must fit to some degree within society. And, thus, society needs standards of behavior to survive. These standards, in the form of shared moral values, allow people to relate to one another and progress in a communal way. They remind us that, while each life is precious and unique, each member of society belongs to a larger whole with obligations to the group at large. Thus, morality becomes a set of road signs and railroad-crossing lights designed to keep each individual moving without impacting adversely on others. For if any society is to be

15

strong and vibrant, its citizens must abide by a common set of rules and understand the shared values of that society

But beyond the benefits for society at large, sound moral conduct enriches the individual as well. Moral values bring structure, dignity, and meaning to our lives. Indeed, if the basic needs of people are met—if they're not starving, if their children have a place to sleep—they generally develop some form of ethical framework very quickly. And as a general rule, highly moral people are happy people. Parents who give their children sound morals bequeath to them the essentials of a happy life. And the higher the moral standard a person has, the better off that person is. For even if one falls short in reaching for an ideal, the act of trying can be a source of fulfillment and an end in itself.

We view moral values as having two separate and distinct components. The first of these deals with order and what the individual owes to society. Rules are necessary for men and women to be free. It might be appealing to have everyone else play by the rules while you are allowed to break them, but anarchy as a whole is an unappealing concept. Thus, sound moral conduct involves mutual adherence to fundamental rules. Thou shalt not kill. Thou shalt not steal. Thou shalt not bear false witness. For only in an atmosphere of reasonable security and order can humanity's best creations grow.

But beyond consideration of what we should

not do, morals also incorporate entitlements, freedoms, and human rights—what society owes the individual. Ours is a nation with beautiful homes, good doctors, fine schools, and every other advantage of contemporary life, but millions of Americans live without them. A moral society must strive for the right of every man and woman to have the opportunity to live a productive fulfilled life. This is not to say that anyone should get something for nothing. When entitlements become unearned and a form of exploiting the system, they breed resentment as someone else's burden and loss. Likewise, personal freedom must be weighed against concern for other people's rights. But morality requires not only that a person live his or her life in a certain way, but also that all of us contribute to a society that strives toward some form of justice for all.

In sum, moral values consist of obligations, responsibilities, freedoms, and rights. And if one seeks to reduce their content to a single thought, the Golden Rule should suffice:

The Confucian Analects 15:23—"What you do not want done to yourself, do not do to others," or Matthew 7:12—"All things whatsoever ye would that men should do to you, do ye even so to them."

The evolution of moral values is a long, slow process, reflecting time-honored beliefs coupled with present-day realities. Some values, such as honesty and charity, have long been regarded as absolute. Others, such as concern for the environment as a moral obligation, have come to promi-

17

nence in recent decades. Moral codes have their greatest force and effect when they express the will of a stable society. And, certainly, in many respects, moral values reflect the conventions of a given society at a particular time rather than a universal standard. For example, thirty years ago, it was considered unacceptable for a sixteen-year-old girl who was pregnant to attend regular classes in high school. Instead, she was sent to a special school with other pregnant students. Now, in many schools, the presence of pregnant students is common and such attendance is widely regarded as preferable for the social development of those students.

Laws are the morals of the body politic; the officially sanctioned moral dictates of the state. There will always be a need for laws as guidelines. But true virtue cannot be commanded. It must come as the result of personal conviction and desire. Moreover, the law is hardly an absolute standard for moral responsibility. Rather, it is the absolute minimum that must be followed. Many acts that are clearly immoral are not against the law. Ethics consists of more than asking a lawyer, "Is it legal?" And in the United States, unlike Islamic countries, we have a minimalist legal system that allows for great latitude in behavior.

Thus, for most people, personal codes are the primary repository for moral values. The law might allow cheating on one's spouse, but the moral code of a responsible individual doesn't. The law allows us to be selfish and self-indulgent, but to many people that type of behavior is wrong. Morality, then, is what goes on between people; not simply a set of rules. And the best morals come from preference and choice. Indeed, were it otherwise, there wouldn't be enough jailers to enforce the rules.

Moral development begins in childhood, and is both psychological and philosophical in content. Some degree of good moral conduct might be innate. But, by and large, values aren't a spontaneous natural product. They must be learned and acquired over time. All infants are selfish at birth. They begin life with a psychology of pure self-interest and no concept of needs other than their own. But as time goes on, they become aware of other people's desires and develop the ability to distinguish right from wrong. Ultimately, they will adhere to some form of moral code for reasons of self-image and self-worth, to obtain approval, respect, and rewards from others, and to avoid punishment and disapproval.

Moral development in children has several prerequisites. The first is early bonding with at least one adult, preferably a parent. Bonding is the emotional connection that allows a child to trust his or her parents, incorporate their wishes in decision making, and understand that doing so won't negate the meeting of that child's own needs.

Next, moral development requires that a child's prerequisites for survival be fulfilled. It's rare to find satisfactory moral development in children who are worried about where their next meal is coming from or whether they'll be sleeping on the street in the cold. Children need a sense that if they behave properly, life will be fair to them in return. Likewise, it's important that a child not be beaten or sexually abused. For, in the words of Langston Hughes, "Those to whom evil is done do evil in return." Unfortunately, though, these evil phenomena have increased markedly in recent years, and they teach children that it's acceptable to use power regardless of the hurt to other people so long as such conduct leads to the abuser's achieving his or her goals.

And last, before children can be expected to do good, they have to understand what and why good is. Thus, moral development is dependent upon inculcating in children the ability to distinguish right from wrong. This requires that children experience what is good, and also that they be exposed to a variety of people, places, and ideas. It's not enough simply to label something as "bad" without explaining why it's wrong. Good moral values require the ability to make a choice. And if children aren't empowered to make real choices regularly, there's no way they'll ever learn.

Parents are generally a child's first moral teachers. Along with extended family, they constitute a child's primary source of values. It is parents who must give a child love and respect—the heart of any moral code—because children who have never known love and respect will find it difficult if not impossible to give love and respect to others. It is parents who must first encourage a child to ask, "What would happen if everyone acted like I'm about to act? Who might be hurt by what I'm about to do?" And it is parents above all others who must be careful to teach not only by word but also by example. They must remember that children, particularly young ones, are seldom able to question what they're learning from their parents, and that poisonous lessons absorbed early in life will filter into a child's psyche long after that child has begun to make value judgments on his or her own.

Beyond parents, moral values come from a variety of sources. We learn from people charged with formal instruction such as teachers in school. Here, the interchange is often one-directional. Someone is charged with the obligation to instruct, and someone else is supposed to learn. We learn values through two-way dialogue with friends and anyone else with whom we exchange ideas. And as we mature, self-analysis and introspection become an important part of moral growth. Indeed, without some form of reflection and introspection, an individual's capacity for moral development is compromised seriously.

For adults as well as children, it's essential to have a framework within which to view moral values. Morals can't be taught piecemeal; they have to relate to a larger whole. For many people, that framework comes from religion. It isn't necessary to define God or give God a gender to have a sense of a Divine being who compels us to carry out certain responsibilities. And believing in God makes it easier for many people to put values in context for themselves. Their faith gives them an all-encompassing value system that eliminates the need to weigh each issue as it arises in terms of family, law, communal good, or some other standard. But whatever the source of a person's ethical framework, life is easier for people who have one. They don't have to decide again and again, "What am I going to do? How do I get around this prohibition?" They have an internal moral compass that points them in the right direction. They simply do what they know to be right.

Still, whatever moral framework a person develops, there's always a zone of individual responsibility and autonomy. Some moral principles go essentially unchallenged. Kindness, generosity, and truth telling are good. Stealing, cheating, and lying are bad. But just as no one is completely happy all of the time, none of us lives a perfectly moral life. We compromise. We develop gaps between what we know to be ideal moral behavior and what we accept in ourselves. Even the most scrupulous among us adjust to a level of comfort with our own conduct. Very few of us put an extra quarter that tumbles out of a pay telephone back into the coin slot. If the cashier in a supermarket gives us too much change, the issue becomes closer. But if we keep the extra quarter that the cashier mistakenly gives us, what happens when one of our children walks out of the same supermarket with a candy bar that hasn't been paid for? How do we explain to eight-year-olds that our conduct in keeping the extra quarter was all right but theirs wasn't? And what if, instead of a quarter, the amount in question is $10?

What do we teach children about crossing the street? Some things are wrong, and then there is crossing against a red light when we're in a hurry and there are no cars in sight. Should the law against jaywalking be regarded as absolute? Are there times, while driving, when it's all right to run a red light? And if so, how will we feel years from now if we get a telephone call saying, "Your son has been killed running a red light"? Will we ask ourselves, "Where did he learn that behavior?"

Even individuals with exacting moral codes inevitably come in contact with blurred lines. Vegetarians who won't wear fur coats often wear leather shoes. There's a tendency on the part of honest individuals to give themselves "the benefit of the doubt" when filling out income tax forms. One guideline for moral behavior is "If you have to lie about it, it's probably wrong." Another is "Don't make that blurred line so convenient and accessible that you abuse it to justify what you know is wrong." But having said all of this, it must be acknowledged that on occasion, moral lines are very difficult to draw. And even on issues of superseding importance, rational, intelligent people of good will can arrive at positions that are diametrically opposed.

The classic example of this is America's current, very painful debate over abortion. Framing the issue from a "pro choice" point of view, the question becomes "Can a society be considered moral if it forces a woman to bear a child she does not want?" But others define the matter in terms of the slaughter of innocent life. And, certainly, there are times when society appropriately forces people to do things that they don't want to do. We force people to go into the armed forces against their will when we have a military draft. We force people to pay taxes whether they want to or not. Thus, clearly, something more than personal preference determines moral obligations.

Our own view on the issue of abortion has been arrived at after much soul-searching and thought. We have looked at abortion in both moral and legal terms. We believe that every abortion is a tragedy, and one of us believes that most abortions are morally wrong. But we also believe in a woman's legal right to significant reproductive freedom.

No life exists in a vacuum. What gives life its greatest meaning is the joy and love experienced in interaction with others and the caring that other people put into each life. We'd like to see a society in which every possibility of human life is welcome; one in which every woman who becomes pregnant chooses to carry her child to term because she would know that, even if she was unable or unwilling to raise her child, there would be others willing and able to do so with proper care and sufficient love. But America today is tragically far from that goal. Many, if not most, unwanted children in this country are ill fed, poorly educated, and raised without adequate medical care. Others, regardless of socioeconomic background, are badly neglected and abused. Too many children grow up in circumstances of hopelessness and despair. And the overwhelming moral issue facing America with regard to abortion today is the extent to which so many women who ideally should look forward to having children look upon pregnancy as an affliction.

We don't think that a woman's right to an abortion is absolute. And we believe that any woman who considers an abortion has an obligation to focus on the reality that there will be consequences to others as a result of her conduct. The duration of her pregnancy, her relationship with her male partner and his feelings, and much more should be taken into account before a final decision is made. Also, the law has to acknowledge that there comes a time when a fetus has developed into a life that must be protected. But our bottom line is, absent appropriate circumstances, society cannot and should not compel a woman to carry a child to term.

Moreover, the moral argument against abortion is weakened at present because many of those who most strenuously oppose abortion haven't put forth a program for a more-nurturing society that would make their position a moral imperative. Morals, as previously noted, don't operate in a vacuum, and no one rule can exist in isolation. Each value must be part of a larger whole. And too many people who argue vociferously for the right of a fetus to be born are unwilling to help that child through life. Society can't deny access to contraception, deny access to abortion, and then, once a child is born, walk away when mother and child are in need. And given America as it presently exists, our view is that the movement to ban abortion—and failing that, to chip away at abortion rights—must present a more compelling alternative for mother and child.

But having said all this, we hasten to add that we don't regard abortion as a litmus test on morality. On some matters, there's a right and a wrong and almost everyone knows what it is. But on the issue of abortion, people of good will who value life greatly and serve society well can make rational moral determinations on either side. And one of the saddest things about America's current abortion debate is that we haven't been able to conduct public discourse without name-calling, ugliness, and anger.

Too often, we judge people on where they come out on a particular issue, without giving them credit for how they deliberated to arrive at their decision. Thus, part of every person's struggle on the issue of abortion and other matters of importance should be: "How can we debate right and wrong, and at the same time, respect differing points of view?" And, in that vein, it must be said that, even when we are confident about our ability to define right and wrong for ourselves, when we start talking about what is right and wrong for other people, we have to give some ground.

Sound moral judgments are oftentimes difficult to arrive at. And maintaining a moral life is never a *fait accompli*. It's a persistent never-ending process of growth, maturity, and change. But, in the end, we believe, the process is worth the effort. For life derives its truest meaning from our relationships with other people. And invariably, when we think of those we know best and love most, what we think most fondly about are the best moral qualities within them.

3

WHAT ARE THE FORCES THAT HAVE IMPACTED ON MORAL VALUES IN THE UNITED STATES IN RECENT DECADES?

AND WHAT ARE THE RESULTS OF THOSE FORCES?

THE UNITED STATES, since its birth, has stood in the forefront of the march for freedom and human rights. The principles enunciated in our Constitution, the Bill of Rights, and other cornerstone documents, while too often limited to white males, were thoughtful and advanced for their time. We have always been a religious nation, albeit without a state religion. And we have always waved a moral flag.

No nation is without blemishes, and the United States has had its share. Slavery and the treatment of Native Americans were repugnant moral failings. The American landscape has been dotted with witch trials, "Red" scares, and other crusades of dubious moral value. But, overall, "American values" have served us well. As a nation, we pioneered free public education, an end to debtors' prisons, Homestead Act land grants, and New Deal entitlements. Immigrants who came to our shores arrived with a sense of opportunity and newfound freedom. We believed in ourselves as a people and as a cohesive society founded on family, community, the workplace, and religion.

But throughout our history, several dark threads have always been interwoven with the gold. One of these threads—violence—has long permeated American culture. Our country was born out of a violent revolution and expanded through violence perpetrated against our native population. In glorifying the Old West and the American frontier, we made heroes, not of farmers who tilled the soil, but of gunfighters, sheriffs, and soldiers. And we remain today a violent country, spawning statistics on weaponry and murder that embarrass us before the world.

Also, the United States is a materialistic country. The accumulation of wealth is a high priority in most societies; we're hardly alone in that regard. But with our emphasis on the status symbol of the moment, be it a new car or hundred-dollar athletic shoes, we appear to be the most materialistic nation in the world. The "American Dream" has always been about wealth; not spiritual strength or happiness. Indeed, progress in America is equated almost exclusively with growth and the extent to which that growth relates to wealth. We use public funds to encourage expansion with relatively little serious planning or consideration of results other than financial return. The development of Southern California is a case in point. Forty years ago, Los Angeles was close to ideal. It was a land of mountains, surf, and orange groves. Now, the city seems to sprawl forever. Travelers flying into Los Angeles International Airport can't see the ground through the smog. Residents spend hours a day in slow-moving automobile traffic. The tension from social pressures is extraordinarily high. And this "progress" is regarded by some as having fallen from the sky, as though no one could see the problems coming.

Perhaps the most painful aspect of America's current moral dilemma is that it didn't have to occur. After the Depression and World War II, American society had only to define its goals and carry them out to be what it wanted to be. In the eyes of most citizens, only two significant problems loomed. One was the battle against Communism, which would drain us throughout the Cold War. And the other was our racial dilemma, which divides us to this day. Both of those problems festered through the late 1940s and 1950s, as America evaluated the hypocrisy of fighting Hitler with segregated troops, debated theories of "separate but equal," fought a war in Korea, and built a nuclear arsenal capable of destroying the world. Then, in the 1960s, they exploded.

The sixties, at their best, represented a quest for the highest possible moral ground. It was an era when principles seemed to matter, and all good things were deemed possible. It's fashionable now to ask what happened to the idealism of the sixties. But a better question might be "How did that idealism occur at all?"

America in the early 1960s felt good about itself. We had defeated the evil German and Japanese empires and, after initial setbacks, pulled even with the Soviet Union in space. We believed as a nation that prosperity was inevitable. The communications revolution, led by television, was making us aware of abuses and inequities in our land, and it seemed only proper to right what was wrong. The era that followed was a watershed for personal freedom, entitlements, and human rights.

The civil rights movement of the sixties represented American morality at its best. Some of the people who got involved might have done so for reasons of personal political ambition. But, for the most part, the men and women who spearheaded the movement—black and white—made enormous sacrifices and took great risks because they cared about doing what was right. It was a giving movement. People like Michael Schwerner, James Chaney, Andrew Goodman, and Viola Liuzzo quite literally laid down their lives in nonviolent fashion because their cause was just.

So, too, aspects of the antiwar movement of the 1960s reflected America's better side. Protesters who marched in antiwar demonstrations waving Vietcong flags missed the point. The Vietcong did not stand for much that the vast majority of "doves" believed in. Rather, the antiwar movement as a whole stood for the proposition that, before killing begins, it's a moral imperative to make certain that the war in question is just. And most Americans who opposed the war did so not because they considered it unwinnable, but for the simple reason that they believed it was wrong.

The 1960s also gave birth to the environmental movement as we know it today. The era marked a turning point in the quest for equal rights for women, homosexuals, the physically disabled, and many others whose rights had been ignored previously. And perhaps most important, for a brief time, there was a serious commitment by the White House, Congress, and the American people to build "The Great Society" that we were capable of constructing. The money appropriated wasn't always well spent; some entitlement programs were hastily conceived and unwise. But America was united in the belief that, when people are mired in poverty and the innocent are suffering, something must be done to help the afflicted, both for their sake and for the sake of society as a whole. Lyndon Johnson put it in very simple terms: "The challenge of the next half-century will be whether we have the wisdom to use our wealth to enrich and elevate our national life and to advance the quality of American civilization. For we have the opportunity to move not only toward the rich society and the powerful society, but upward to The Great Society."

This was a true effort to construct "a kinder, gentler America." But the going got tough. John Kennedy, Malcolm X, Robert Kennedy, and Martin Luther King, Jr., were assassinated within a span of four and a half years. And, with their deaths, a crucial underpinning of America's value system was

35

shaken. Faith in the political process and the power of moral appeals had been crushed by violence. The war in Vietnam dragged on. The poverty didn't go away. Racial tensions continued to build, exploding in the North in the form of urban riots. America learned that it couldn't do everything it thought it could do. And though television had opened our eyes to the horrors of poverty, racism, and war, we eventually lost heart and became anesthetized to it all.

Also, although the 1960s might have been a golden era in defining what society owes the individual in terms of entitlements, freedom, and human rights, it was far less effective in defining what the individual owes to society. Every man and woman who enjoys the benefits of a social system has an obligation to that system and its other participants. No one should consciously act in a manner that weakens the fabric of society. Yet, in the mid and late 1960s, Americans sometimes seemed to forget that freedom is accompanied by obligations, and that responsibilities are a natural corollary to rights. Tolerance as a positive value was abused and came to justify an absence of moral standards. Too many people from across socioeconomic lines began chanting a three-word mantra for social action: "You owe me." The rights of individuals within society became confused with "rights" against society, and respect and support for authority waned.

Neither of us believes in authority for its own sake. Both of us believe firmly in democracy. We don't think that authority should set America's moral agenda. But when authority is toppled, it has to be replaced with something—preferably, a set of consensus values. And in the United States, since the 1960s, we've steadfastly avoided honest debate—as opposed to political posturing—about what those consensus values should be. This phenomenon of losing authority without substituting an alternative source of responsible behavior has been an enormous moral loss. And the problem has been exacerbated by a number of trends that have plagued our society in recent years.

The most basic of these trends is the breakdown of the family. All children are better off with positive parental involvement in their lives, and as a general rule, they experience serious deprivation when that involvement is missing. Parents and extended family are the first teachers and the first heroes that virtually all children have. Yet, more and more children today are growing up in one-parent homes, no-parent homes, homes with two working parents, and other situations that have deprived them of the presence of concerned relatives much of the time. For many children, the extended family has all but disappeared. Children today are more alone in America than ever before.

Moreover, even when parents are present physically, there is often a lack of quality interaction between parent and child. Children need someone who will listen to them, and also someone they can listen to. And this is particularly true in an age when children have far more to contend with than their counterparts of thirty or forty years ago. They're regularly put into situations in which they must make choices regarding sex and drugs. They're unsure of the value of the skills that they will develop by working hard in school. They're told that, in many ways, they will have less than their parents and that their expectations should diminish accordingly. Yet, at the same time, many parents are so busy with other pursuits that they don't have time, or don't take the time when they do come home, to sit and talk with their children.

This problem cuts across class lines. It's not just an inner-city dilemma. Oftentimes, wealthy parents have very needy children. In many infants' rooms today, there are expensive toys, furniture, clothes—but no parent. As children get older, their parents find it seductively easy to sit them down in front of a television set and pretend they're taking care of them. By age sixteen, many children have keys to a car and money to hang out at a local shopping mall, but still no parental guidance. And in many respects, these children are as neglected as the welfare baby in Harlem or Watts.

"Where did we go wrong?" a child's parents might ask when he or she gets in trouble. "We gave him everything." But did they give him attention? Was there day-to-day contact and discipline? Was there a parent who said, "Yes, I had a hard day at work today, but I still have an hour to talk with you. What's on your mind? What happened to you today? Do you have homework? Where are you going when you go out tonight? Who are you going with? I want you home by ten o'clock."

A generation ago, within the family, most people understood their responsibilities and roles. But that's simply not the case anymore. It's possible to teach morality without bedrock family support. Were the situation otherwise, orphans could never have good moral values, and many orphans are quite moral. But it's harder without family, particularly without parents. And at the same time the American family has been breaking down, the community values that once buttressed morality have also been disintegrating.

The overriding constant of the twentieth century has been change. Once, people were born in a community, grew up, worked, married, raised children, matured, and died—all within a few miles of where they were born. Communities bred shared values, a sense of identity, and a feeling of belonging. Neighbors on porches or building stoops watched after each other's children. And if a child did something wrong, it was of concern to the whole neighborhood, it wasn't just a family problem

However, in recent decades, society has become very mobile, busy, and large. Americans now often work many miles from home and pull up roots from time to time. Mothers, who once served as the backbone of community organizations and volunteerism, are now in the workforce in paying jobs. On occasion, communities still unite around a winning football team or a shared natural disaster. But significant values are rarely developed and seldom discussed in a community setting anymore. Moral lapses go unnoticed in the anonymity of the crowd.

Yet even as this country finds itself in need of

more shared values, common experiences, and standards, Americans see their communities being further divided by doubts about our common heritage and a tide of "multiculturalism," particularly along racial lines. Immigrants traditionally came to the United States to forge a common identity with other Americans. It worked for most, but not for all. And it certainly didn't work for black Americans, who were brought here in chains and, centuries later, subjected to the presumption that integration should mean the eradication of what was left of black culture; that black values should be replaced by white.

Race, not religion or class, has always been the primary dividing factor in America. Now, more than ever before, America seems in danger of racial fragmentation, and this racial dilemma goes directly to the heart of values that we as Americans have been taught to cherish. Instead of uniting behind what we have in common, the view has begun to predominate that ethnic groups should take pride primarily in the achievements of their "own kind." Respect for America's multicultural heritage has given way to an emphasis on *different* heritages. Too often now, issues of right and wrong are subjugated to race, with bigotry and profiteering on all sides. Black racism has become as pernicious as white racism; so much so that some leaders of the civil rights movement in America today have lost the moral high ground to which they once had legitimate claim.

An end to America's racial dilemma will

come only through tolerance, mutual understanding, compromise, and respect. Justice will be one requisite component of a solution; forgiveness, another. We will not build a better society through hatred, fear, and violence. Those in power will have to realize that the status quo must change, and that people need self-identity and an understanding of self for their values to flourish. We recognize the fact that many minority Americans have been taught little about themselves in school. They know next to nothing about their history. And the history of Africa, Latin America, and Asia is as important to cultural identity as the history of Europe. But the primary obligation of responsible citizens is to unite rather than to divide. Democracy can't work without a common cultural base that is understood and appreciated by all. And to reject the tradition of our Founding Fathers, modeled as it was on Western culture and the ideals of the Enlightenment, simply because all fifty-six signers of the Declaration of Independence were white males is wrong. Thus, we believe that a variety of cultures should be explored in school, but with an emphasis on common unifying factors. Then each person will be able to contribute to our national identity, and a sense of community supportive of shared values can flourish.

In addition to the breakdown of family and community structure, moral values in America have also been affected by the diminishing influence of religion in the *private* life of our citizenry.

In America's formative years, most people

41

believed that ultimately they would be judged by God. And God was not a synonym for the laws of nature or a structured moral code. He was an all-powerful creator, who knew each person's deeds and the motives behind them. Men and women felt compelled to conform their behavior to His will, and while there might have been struggles over precisely what that will was, because of their belief in God's omnipotence, the majority of Americans lived their lives mindful of a master moral plan.

But morality in twentieth-century America has lost its supernatural underpinning. We have televangelists who purport to tell us what God wants us to do. We have fundamentalists who scour the political landscape in an effort to make government and religion coincide. But in the privacy of our homes, where it matters most, an ever-decreasing number of Americans feel they are being watched by God. The concept of a soul's being readied for final judgment as a motivating force for righteous behavior has been severely diminished. And having lost that faith, many men and women have lost the force that anchored their moral code.

Television has also contributed to America's changing moral climate. At its best, TV is capable of entertaining and informing in remarkable fashion. Certain issues, such as the plight of the homeless, have been brought to the fore as a consequence of media coverage. And major events such as the Persian Gulf War and congressional Watergate hearings are often handled well. But in many respects, as far as television is concerned, negatives abound.

Perhaps the most important thing to understand about television in America is that it is an institution run almost entirely for financial gain. In other words, virtually every brain in America has been wired into a marketing device designed to sell products, not ideas. Also, while the information explosion that began with television has given us the illusion of understanding, oftentimes there is little depth to our perceptions. Events on TV in the form of "sound bites" are frequently isolated from a larger whole. Because the medium is run for profit, there is constant pressure on each new program to go a bit further than the one before. More sex; more violence; more killing, more gruesomely done. Instead of encouraging people to go out and do things, TV encourages them to watch passively at home. And all of this is magnified when it comes to the impact of television on children.

Children are extraordinary receivers of information, and rarely question what they see on television. Instead, they accept it virtually whole, and the TV in their home is a powerful force in their lives. To a degree, this is true of the music industry as well, but television reaches considerably further in molding young people's character. And few things are more disheartening than watching what many children see on television, particularly on Saturday morning.

Take a three-year-old. Put him in front of a television. Start him off with cartoons showing people being pushed over cliffs, going *splat*, and re-forming into people again. Then let that child graduate to Rambo, heads being blown away, and a stream of killing for ten more years. Is it any wonder that this child at age thirteen will have a callous attitude toward violence and human life?

By and large, the content of television is far below what we should be reaching for. It makes behavior without standards seem attractive, humiliates sensitivity, and besieges children with greed, violence, vulgarity, and sex out of context. It takes children away from reading, thinking, playing, and otherwise interacting in quality fashion with adults and their peers. It deprives parents of their right and obligation to choose which ideas are pressed upon their sons and daughters. And the truth is, in this day and age, it's virtually impossible to separate children from television. You might be able to keep television out of your house, but all that means is that your children will spend less time at home because they'll be over at a friend's house watching television.

The decline of our schools—particularly our public schools—has also contributed to falling moral standards. Some schools are communities, but others are little more than architectural structures. Many students and teachers have lost respect for one another. Often, they think of their school building as a benign form of prison. Within the classroom, matters of right and wrong are seldom discussed. And where once parents relied on school to reaffirm moral values for their children, now there's often concern regarding what their children shouldn't learn in school, starting with the wrong lessons about illegal drugs. These drugs, which are easily obtained in virtually every public high school in America, further contribute to the moral abyss that our society is in. They destroy individual initiative, create crime, and subvert the work culture. Once addicted, physically or psychologically, a person finds that his or her drug of choice has become a value in and of itself.

And in recent decades, all of the aforementioned problems have been compounded by the loss of quality political leadership in America. Governing well requires intelligence, independence, integrity, compassion, and courage. Yet , we find ourselves mired in a political process that rewards manipulation, lying, the absence of moral standards, and pandering to the lowest common denominator.

Politics in America today is brought to us by television, with illusion and deceit substituted for reality. Oftentimes, candidates don't even say what they think. They say what media advisers tell them to say in order to reap the gains of sound bites on the evening news. Rather than act in accord with honestly held beliefs, they rely upon opinion polls to distinguish "right" from "wrong." Getting elected is the ultimate value; an end in itself, not the means to a better end.

In years past, when politicians made promises, at least they tried to keep them. Now, often, they make promises and move on without even trying to fulfill their part of the bargain with the public at large. Everything has become a deal. The political process is dominated by wealth. Many of our legislative bodies have less turnover in representation than one finds in totalitarian governments. And when there is change in representation, it seems to be only because the money has turned over.

Obviously, there are still good people in public service today. Many of the men and women in government are dedicated, caring, competent individuals with a clear sense of the public trust. But too many people in government jobs are takers, and the system is structured to accommodate them. We read in history books about the legendary Tweed Courthouse as "a monument to graft and corruption." But "Boss Tweed" and his underlings misappropriated far less than those who plunder the public treasury today. And in days past, at least political corruption was recognized as such. Now government officials put campaign workers in no-show jobs, legislators take substantial contributions in return for access and other favors, and somehow the appropriate enforcement tribunals—frequently ethics committees in the same legislative bodies—almost always fall short of finding their conduct to be unlawful. We elect officials to important jobs, and the day after election, they're using their newly-won position as a platform to run for higher office. What

does that say about the view of these "public ser-
vants" toward the public trust? In sum, too few
political leaders today inspire the belief that their
reason for seeking office is to advance the public
good. Indeed, to the contrary, what we seem to
have now is politics without regard for the public
good. And that problem is particularly acute at the
national level, extending to the presidency itself.

Many of our country's presidents have been
marginal. For every giant like George Washington
or Abraham Lincoln, there has been a Harding,
Fillmore, or Grant. Greatness does not necessarily
come with the office. But the 1980s witnessed a
profoundly disturbing trend that went beyond the
inadequacies of previous administrations. Presidents Ronald Reagan and George Bush both talked
of the need to restore values and principles in our
society. But in reality they seemed to promote near-
total indifference to moral standards and issues of
ethical conduct, placing power and privilege
above the needs of the people.

Reagan helped mold a political climate that
enabled affluent transgressors to run wild. Bend-
ing and breaking the rules became acceptable.
There was deregulation in many areas, a systematic weakening of enforcement provisions, and
underfunding of the enforcers who were supposed to monitor behavior in white-collar sectors
of the economy. "Special interests" might have
been savaged in the political process, but selfish
interests were allowed to flourish in the govern-
mental arena. Permissive "liberal" ideologies were

attacked, but supposedly conservative ideologies bordering in many instances on economic plunder were encouraged. In a sense, the scandals that followed were inevitable. But, beyond that, Ronald Reagan and George Bush seemed determined to embrace platitudes in lieu of necessary government action and to take government out of the business of governing. They all but ignored the tasks of educating our citizenry, ensuring the integrity of our financial system, preserving our infrastructure, maintaining a reasonably clean environment, providing adequate health care, and, perhaps most important, securing equal opportunity for every American. In response, the Democrats in Congress did a poor job of being a competent party in opposition. For the most part, they were inept, splintered, and scared. And now that we have a Democratic administration and a Republican Congress, we foresee little improvement in the near future.

We're tired of leaders who pontificate about America as "the land of opportunity," when in fact that opportunity is minimal if not entirely lacking for many members of America's underclass. We're tired of leaders who talk a lot about traditional family values as a campaign tactic, but do almost nothing to help sustain the American family. And we're tired of leaders who, in recent years, have moved virtually every major policy decision on the federal level away from the development of human resources. For too long, the attention of the White House was focused on those who already

had it made, rather than on those in need. We had
a decade-plus of presidents who believed that
those in positions of economic power had
"earned" that power regardless of whether it came
to them through hard work, inheritance, or luck.
These presidents might have talked to the disadvantaged and offered encouragement. But they
consistently refused to use government to assist
the underclass in any meaningful fashion. They
never tackled issues of need in the way these
issues had to be attacked. Instead, the message
heard by disadvantaged Americans was "If you
make it, great; I'll be on your side. But I'm not
going to help you get to where you want to be."
And as a consequence of that philosophy, at the
close of 1992, 35.7 million Americans, more than at
any time since 1964, when Lyndon Johnson
declared his "War on Poverty," were living "below
the poverty line." And the richest one percent of
American households owned 36 percent of the
nation's privately held property, while the bottom
90 percent shared 32 percent of the wealth. Not
since the eve of the Great Depression has the dis-
parity between rich and poor in this country been
more sharply defined.

Moreover, for twelve years, we had presidents
who refused to admit failure in critical areas, and
consistently maintained that the problems plagu-
ing our society simply didn't exist. Entire cities
filed for bankruptcy. Three million people became
homeless. Our health care and educational systems
fell into disarray. The federal budget deficit grew

to exceed $400 billion annually, notwithstanding laws that mandated deficit reduction. In the span of twelve years, we were transformed from the largest creditor nation to the largest debtor nation in the world. We mortgaged our future, fiscally and environmentally. And what did we get in exchange for this multi-trillion-dollar debt? Did we retrain America's workforce? Revitalize our inner cities? Repair our nation's crumbling infrastructure? To the contrary, the White House did essentially nothing about these problems. Instead, it reduced political debate to thirty-second sound bites about Willie Horton, the Pledge of Allegiance, and other trivia having little to do with the major issues facing America. Flying the American flag is admirable. Using it as a blanket to cover over problems is not. Yet for twelve years, style and political charm were employed as substitutes for substantive national leadership. Our presidents excelled at proclaiming lofty goals, but never before had we suffered leaders so intransigent and irresponsible in failing to set standards of accountability. They lacked the courage to tell us the truth. For all practical purposes, they refused to give us bad news of any kind. Perhaps they led us to feel better as a nation, but we didn't become better. And that feeling was a cruel illusion because, like the student who graduates from school with a diploma but can't read, our harsh truth lay ahead.

But to lay all the blame for the failure of American political leadership on the White House, Congress, or any level of government would absolve the American people of a responsibility that all of us share. For just as no system of government is better than the people who run it, public officials are rarely better than the people who elect them. Morals don't "trickle down" from the top, any more than wealth does. And, overall, our leaders' values reflect what has happened to our society as a whole. We are the ones who put these candidates in the political arena and elect and reelect them to office. And when all is said and done, we don't seem to care a whole lot if they're hypocrites, liars, or frauds.

Let a simple example suffice. On July 6, 1991, George Bush announced the nomination of Clarence Thomas to the United States Supreme Court, and declared, "The fact that he is black and a minority had nothing to do with this." Laying aside the redundancy of Bush's statement, it was simply not true. To think otherwise would be akin to following Alice down the rabbit hole into a bizarre wonderland. Indeed, it's hard to believe that any American, including Justice Thomas's most ardent supporters, thought that race had nothing to do with his nomination.

All of us know that lying is wrong. It's an insult to be lied to. Yet, George Bush did it, apparently in the belief that he wouldn't be held accountable by the American people for his lie.

Why? Perhaps because we lie to ourselves. We have become a nation of excusers and justifiers, rather than people who demand that our leaders, our families, our peers, each and every one of us, adhere to adequate standards of moral behavior. And the result of our failure to demand such standards is painfully clear.

We are witnessing the disintegration of social organization in America. Once, there were multiple sources of sound values for individuals. Families, schools, religious institutions, and community organizations were separate in many aspects, but they were part of an overall framework within which each person strove to be morally whole. Now, too often, these institutions operate without reference to one another and with no purpose other than their own separate interests. Thus, the cohesive setting in which people acquired and maintained values no longer exists. We no longer share a common set of rules. And the consequence has been not a movement toward independence or personal freedom, but a breakdown of standards and values.

Society today encourages the development of lives without reflection. The pace is fast, with a premium on instant gratification and quick solutions. Everything is "push button." Our children, in particular, live in a world with virtually no links to the past. And because they don't understand or seem to appreciate what happened yesterday, they have no sense of what should happen tomorrow.

Our parents seem like period pieces in terms of how they valued morals. Issues of honesty and fair dealing, which were important to them, aren't as weighted anymore. Fewer and fewer people say, "Even though it's to my advantage, I won't do this because it's wrong." Indeed, many people, and particularly children, don't even see their acts within the context of right and wrong. Whether they're "wilding" in New York's Central Park or engaging in other forms of antisocial behavior, they feel no remorse and fail completely to relate what they're doing to society as a whole. There's no guilt; no sense of what it might be like to be that other person they're hurting. Just self-interest: "I'm entitled to do whatever I want regardless of the consequences to others. What will make *me* feel good now?"

There's nothing wrong with pursuing individual goals. This nation prospered because of a strong belief in individuality. But like our institutions that have dried up morally, many Americans today serve only themselves. They're locked in social systems, from corporate boardrooms to inner-city streets, where being principled isn't rewarded and sometimes even is punished. Their values have been put through a meat grinder of social permissiveness and greed. And, ultimately, people either opt out of those systems or they are corrupted by them.

Violence still permeates our society in the form of murder, battered women, child abuse, and other assaults. We own more guns than any other people on earth. In six states and the District of Columbia, more people are killed by gunfire than die in automobile accidents each year. Yet for many young men growing up, life is incomplete until they get a gun. There's a constitutional debate over whether Americans should be allowed to own state-of-the-art submachine guns. In 1991, there were 677 murders in Canada and 24,703 in the United States; and one-sixth of the murders in the United States were committed by teenagers.

Like violence, materialism is still a hallmark of our culture. There is extraordinary suffering on Earth. Each year, millions of babies starve to death before they reach the age of one. Typhoons rage through Bangladesh, and drought grips northern Africa. Here at home, we see seventy-year-old women asleep on the streets beside sacks of belongings that most of us would consider trash. And, at the same time, Michael Milken uses his energy and imagination to create a personal income of $500 million in one year. Donald Trump is adored for his wealth. Greed is equated with public policy, subjugating national goals to private ends.

We're dangerously out of control with our materialism; the way in which we've been conditioned and driven to want things. The new car, the new television, new jewelry, new clothes. The quality of our lives has come to be measured by the possessions we own and how much money we're making. Possessions are more important to many than being part of a family or community. Accumulation and hoarding are as appreciated by the public as sharing and charity. When we look at our classmates at a high school reunion, the ones who are considered successful are the ones who are rich. How they got there, what they did to earn

their money, whether or not they're in happy mar-
riages, seems largely irrelevant. We rate people's
lives, not by the good they've done, not by how
happy they are, but by their wealth and, where
applicable, their celebrity status. We've become a
society that trivializes moral judgments in pursuit
of the credo "What's in it for me?" Most often, the
rewards we seek are measured in material terms.
But regardless of the payoff, "me too" has become
"me first" and, where possible, "me only." There's
little commitment beyond self-pleasure and let's
make a dollar. In the 1960s, our moral conscious-
ness was raised by leaders like Martin Luther
King, Jr., and John and Robert Kennedy. But who
articulates values for America today? Donald
Trump? Michael Jordan? Madonna? Talk to children about why they shouldn't cheat in school,
and often they'll look at you as though it's the first
time they've heard that message. Volunteerism
strikes them as a strange phenomenon. Other people's feelings are regarded as trivial.

Walk the streets of our major cities. It used to
be that when someone bumped into you, they'd
stop and say "Excuse me." Now, as often as not,
they glare. Cars run red lights. Pedestrians
unwrap candy bars and throw the wrappers,
along with whatever else they no longer want, on
the sidewalk. It's wrong to throw a candy-bar
wrapper on the sidewalk. And beyond that, it's
symbolic of a decline in civility and the erosion of
simple moral judgments. The person who litters
might be saying, "I'm a slob; my home is a mess;

pride in appearance and cleanliness simply aren't values that I've been taught." Or they might be saying, "I litter because of my disdain for society, or because I'm lazy." But regardless, the person who litters says, "I'm not going to obey the law." And across the board, too many people in the United States no longer obey the law. They disobey it in little ways—littering and running red lights (which becomes more significant if there's an accident)—and in big ways, such as armed robbery or committing stock fraud.

"Society is impossible," Thomas Huxley once wrote, "unless those who are associated agree to observe certain rules of conduct toward one another. Its stability depends on the steadiness with which they abide by that agreement." Yet it doesn't take a majority of the population to break the law for the law to not work. If a significant minority decides to transgress, the law will ultimately fail. And what has happened now in America is that enough people are breaking the law that law enforcement is breaking down. People justify breaking the law the same way they justify other immoral conduct. They say, "That's the way the system really works," or "Everybody does it if they can." Perhaps they tell themselves that they're "evening out the inequities of life." Or sometimes they simply do what they want without any attempt to justify their behavior at all.

How do people who break the law get that way? We've talked about some of the factors that have led to the erosion of moral values in America—the breakdown of families, the disintegration of communities, the diminishing influence of religion in private life, the impact of television, the decline of our public schools, drugs (and alcohol abuse), the loss of quality political leadership. These factors operate throughout society. And among the disadvantaged, they are compounded by substandard or no housing, unemployment, illiteracy, malnutrition, inadequate health care from womb to grave, exposure to random violence, powerlessness before established institutions, hatred, fear, hopelessness, and injustice.

The United States has always had an underclass. But in recent decades, we've seen an underclass that has fallen below the minimum social and economic standards acceptable in a prosperous society. It's not just "below the poverty level." It's a disaster that threatens to become a permanent way of life for millions of people and their progeny for generations to come.

Obviously, there are many disadvantaged Americans—a clear majority—who don't use environment as an excuse to engage in violence or other antisocial conduct. They understand that, although their surroundings might offer an explanation, environment isn't a justification for crime or other immoral behavior. But moral values tend to fall when people feel victimized by circumstances beyond their control. And in many parts of our country today, ills of the human spirit and ills of the human condition coincide. Indeed, many neighborhoods in our cities have become so unlivable that we might soon be forced to look toward Third World countries as models for solutions.

This crisis is particularly acute among black Americans, and strikes with particular fury against the young. America's black elite may be better off now than it was twenty-five years ago. But, in many respects, the majority of black Americans have been subjected to worsening conditions. Two-thirds of all black births in the United States today are out of wedlock. Fifty-seven percent of all black children under the age of eighteen live with a single parent who has never been married. The life expectancy for a black male born in Harlem is shorter than that of a child born in Bangladesh. Homicide is the leading cause of death for black men between the ages of fifteen and thirty-four. Blacks comprise 12 percent of our population but almost half of all murder victims. Twenty-three percent of all black American men in their twenties are in jail, on probation, or on parole. The national high school dropout rate for black students is roughly one in five. Forty-three percent of all black children in the United States live in poverty.

The factors that impel teenagers to go "wilding" in Central Park are different in many respects from those that create white-collar crime. Just as wealthy bankers are disinclined to mug elderly women on the street, inner city adolescents rarely violate provisions of the Securities Exchange Act of 1934. But no one can dispute the fact that, when children grow up in abject poverty amidst violence and deprivation, it's difficult for them to care about much beyond their own survival and instant gratification. And while a child with the luck to be born into a functional family in a cohesive neighborhood with viable schools is likely to form solid core values, too many of our children have no such good fortune. Rather, they suffer from an absence of hope and no sense that good deeds will be rewarded. The media build their resentment and whet their appetite for material possessions they can't afford. At a time when many adolescents are ignored by their parents, schools, and religious institutions, advertisers pay a lot of attention to them, and the message preached is "You are what you own." Society spends more money inculcating in them a desire to own expensive athletic shoes than it does on their health care. Violence periodically enters their lives with no rhyme, reason, or order. At least America's turn-of-the-century vigilantes—and no attempt is made here to justify their actions—had a code that they purported to be enforcing. Today's perpetrators of violence act with no rules or values at all.

But the moral erosion and criminal conduct that plague America are in no way bound by class. "One of the persistent delusions of mankind," Bertrand Russell has written, "'is that some sections of the human race are morally better or worse than others. This belief has many different forms, none of which has any rational basis."

Thus, crime in America has many faces. Street crime, committed largely by our nation's underclass, is one of them. "Organized crime," run by the Mafia and other criminal enterprises, is another. But white-collar crime—in the form of stock fraud, price fixing, embezzlement, tax evasion, and other systematic violations of statutes and regulatory codes—is perhaps the most costly criminal conduct of all. And even when the members of America's business elite conform to the law, they often act as though morality is a costly luxury they can't afford.

One of the saddest developments in American life today is that business can rarely be done on a handshake anymore. In the past, a person's word was his or her bond. Now, the diminished value of that word reflects our loss of trust in each other. An all-too-frequent attitude in business is "I'll breach the contract; I'll skirt the regulation. The worst that can happen to me is, I'll be forced to repay ill-gotten gains or pay what I should have paid in the first place." Bankruptcy, where financially advantageous, isn't avoided. If it's not illegal, it's okay; just another business strategy. Indeed, moral standards in business and elsewhere have fallen so badly and seem so irretrievably lost that oftentimes people campaign not to restore those standards but to justify the change.

In the "old days," Americans might have wanted to be rich, but they also wanted to earn their fortunes. They created tangible empires and manufactured essential products. Now, a "money culture" has replaced our industrial economy, and great fortunes are amassed on paper. Few internal standards are applied to business activity other than the likelihood of generating profit, which oftentimes appears only on a magnetic tape or computer screen. The former chief executive officer and president of Salomon Brothers told us about their moral values in the way they dealt with United States Treasury auctions. Other white-collar entrepreneurs, who enjoyed every advantage America has to offer, devastated the savings and loan industry.

Too few corporate executives counsel their employees: "We will forgo improved financial performance in favor of doing what is right." Whenever "right" becomes an issue, it's unlikely to be perceived in terms other than a corporation's obligation to its shareholders—except when a hostile takeover threatens entrenched executives' jobs. The law is manipulated and twisted, so that loopholes become the letter and spirit of the law. And, on occasion, the law is deliberately broken in the manner of a basketball team's taking an intentional foul: "We'll pay the price if we get caught and happily go on doing business, having gained the advantage we sought."

Suppose you're the chief executive officer of a major oil company. Your company uses single-hull ships when it could use double-hull vessels to avoid a major environmental disaster. The double-hull ships cost more. All too often today, CEOs will say: "We're playing by the rules. If we pollute criminally, prosecute us. If we do it negligently, sue us. We're abiding by the laws of the society in which we live." But where does morality fit in? What is that CEO's vision of the world? How big a risk is he willing to take for corporate financial gain? And what about the president of a tobacco company, who maintains there's no hard evidence that cigarette smoking increases the risk of lung cancer or other diseases despite persuasive proof developed by the company's own scientists that hundreds of thousands of Americans die prematurely each year as a consequence of cigarette smoking? Simply put, at the level at which these individuals are functioning and can do the most for society, they're failing. They haven't lived up to their moral obligations, obligations that go beyond the laws that corporate America has been able to shape and manipulate through lobbying and political action. And even though their companies might give money to charity, donate computers to inner-city schools, and provide jobs in troubled economic times, what they're doing is wrong.

The sad fact of the matter is that, in recent years, more and more white-collar professions have abandoned traditions of behavior that evolved over the lifetime of our country. Consider, for example, the legal profession. Both of us—the authors of this book—are attorneys. One of us clerked for a federal judge and practiced with a prominent Wall Street law firm. The other is now dean of a respected law school. And we're troubled by the values we see today among lawyers.

There have always been scoundrels who practiced law. But in years past, there was a pretty clear dichotomy between them and the rest of the legal profession. Honorable attorneys knew who the scoundrels were, and by and large stayed away from them. Now, the legal profession as a whole has virtually given up on the concept of the bar's being a special culture that adheres to a higher-than-normal standard of ethics. Some attorneys still believe and practice that philosophy, but their numbers are dwindling.

The power of the law today is most often concentrated in large law firms. It's a secondary power, an agent's power. But these big firms are among the engines that move society, and too few lawyers who practice in them look to public service beyond billable hours. Overall, the majority of lawyers have become businessmen, using their craft to make as much money as they can with no higher ethical standards than any other segment of the population. Partly, this might be because different people are now entering the profession. Years ago, law wasn't the way to get rich. The most economically successful individuals in a community rarely were lawyers. Now, because economics have changed, many of the most aggressive, brightest, greediest people in the country have turned to law, often in conjunction with investment banking.

Lawyers are interesting thinkers, particularly when litigating. The adversarial system of American justice means that they live in a world where they can dance on either side of issues and debate anything. They justify virtually every position they take and whatever means they use on grounds that they're simply doing what's best for their clients. And this allows them to disassociate from larger issues of right and wrong.

In order to be good within the rules of the

game, lawyers often have to be manipulative. But beyond that, as with politics, for many attorneys lying has become an accepted part of the legal process. Truth and justice take a backseat to the ultimate value of winning. Client and counsel reinforce one another in "forgetting" crucial facts and "lying like a lawyer." How often is a witness indicted for perjury after testifying falsely at a deposition or trial? Almost never! Virtually everything is up for grabs on Lady Justice's ethical scales. And in the legal profession, as elsewhere in America's corporate culture, it's extremely difficult to succeed if one takes a moral position and by doing so swims against the tide of one's peers.

Neither of us has the ability to judge what goes on in another person's soul; and neither of us will try. But we do have the ability to see thoughts reduced to action. We can make judgments regarding conduct. And looking at our country today, we see a nation that appears dangerously close to emulating what might be analogized to a "big bang theory" of social evolution. At times, it appears as though we've expanded as far as we can as a society and are now in danger of imploding. Indeed, there are moments when, given our myriad domestic crises, one can envision a worst-case scenario in which the United States becomes the "pitiful helpless giant" that Richard Nixon invoked to prolong our involvement in Vietnam. Only we can no longer blame our problems on a worldwide Communist conspiracy or some other external entity. They are of our own making, right here at home.

In his second inaugural address, Franklin Roosevelt told the nation, "We have always known that heedless self-interest was bad morals. We know now that it is bad economics." Roosevelt's words are as true today as they were during the Great Depression. We know now that science cannot replace ethics in eliminating hunger, disease, and poverty. We know that human nature remains flawed. And we should have learned that, for our nation as a whole, good moral values are cost-effective. But more than that, they are a necessity for national survival. And moral issues are more critical than ever today because of the stakes involved. The world is moving very fast, and mistakes are exponentially more costly than before. With the world economy interlinked, a single major financial scandal has repercussions for us all. The devastation caused by one Chernobyl-type environmental catastrophe or one errant nuclear weapon can shatter tens of millions of lives. Once we cut down all the rain forests in the Amazon Basin, they can never be restored. A hole that expands in the ozone layer will exist forevermore. Our nation and the world are no longer so large that we can hide all our mistakes and flaws. And with all these concerns, we must also feed, house, clothe, and educate an ever-increasing army of the poor as history moves on.

These issues can be addressed successfully only if we, as a nation, understand that there is a morality that encompasses them all. Some thoughts on how to teach that understanding follow in the next chapter.

4

HOW CAN WE AS A SOCIETY INSTILL BETTER VALUES?

I<small>T WOULD BE</small> nice if there were a simple formula that we could use to instill better moral values in people. A button to push; a magic potion to drink. But there isn't. To the contrary, it takes discipline, decency, creativity, sacrifice, and an understanding of how values must be put to use to promote the public good—qualities that have been in short supply in recent years. The 1980s, in particular, provided poor soil for moral growth. Too often, Americans sought easy solutions and personal gain with someone else paying the price. Indeed, at times, the era seemed to be personified by the maxim "Everybody wants to go to heaven, but nobody wants to die."

Whether the 1990s provide more fertile soil will be determined in the years ahead. Meanwhile, though, it's important to remember that there are millions of Americans who do live highly principled lives. They recognize their obligation to act ethically and bequeath a sound moral framework to future generations. These men and women do their best to distinguish right from wrong and do what is right. And if America is to flourish in the coming decades, it must follow the example set by these individuals.

Any attempt to instill better values in our society, by definition, should start with children. It's not easy to change a person's character as he or she grows older: "The Child is father of the Man." But children who learn sound morals early in life have less to learn and unlearn later on.

Childhood's "early years" are shorter now than before. Children today are often called upon to make choices and judgments in a complex, confusing world. It's also more difficult to be a good parent now than in the past, but certain essentials remain unchanged.

All children have within them the capacity for good and bad acts, and their capacity for good must be nurtured. That means a child should be guided, praised, corrected, and loved. Love is the most important prerequisite. It has to do with connections between people. But children also need something larger than themselves, a set of ideals to believe in and flow into. And, in that regard, the best thing parents can do for their children is to teach by example; show their children how to live an ethical life. Parents must also be willing to impose rules on children. Not just rules that are easy to enforce, but rules that encourage children to take responsibility for their behavior. Ultimately, each child should believe: "Every time I know the difference between right and wrong, and have a choice, and choose to do what's right, I've grown a little."

As we know, though, many children don't have parents who pay attention to their moral development, and we can't simply walk away from those children. And even when parents do care, they often need more support than is available from established institutions. Indeed, one of the great ironies of the 1990s is that at the same time we're being told with increasing certainty by social scientists exactly what children need in order to develop good morals, an increasing number of children are being deprived of the same. The very institutions that parents once relied upon in the joint effort to teach values are failing. And the task before us now is twofold: (1) to restore those institutions; and (2) where that isn't possible, find other institutions to pick up the slack.

We'd like to see this effort receive bedrock support in our schools. In order for people to care about the difference between right and wrong, they have to have a stake in society. And no one can feel fully enfranchised, nor will we be able to help them adequately, if they can't read, write, and perform basic mathematical skills. Education is the key to life. We have to educate people to a reasonable level. And that includes adequate funding for "head start" programs, as well as an end to barriers that keep homeless children out of school. In addition, we need more social agencies playing an active role in school. In many areas of our country, convicted murderers in prison enjoy better health care and nutrition than children. School is the one place where most of our children can be found. And school is where we should make certain that children receive proper medical care, balanced meals, after-class supervision, and whatever else they need to thrive.

But equally important, we believe that schools, both public and private, should play a more active role in the moral development of children. In recent years, schools in America have become places of accommodation rather than a source of values. The decision by various school boards to distribute condoms is a case in point. The rationale for distribution is that students are having sex anyway, and giving them condoms will reduce pregnancies and the spread of venereal disease, most notably AIDS. But the other side of the coin is that school officials are, in effect, telling children, "It's all right for you to have sexual intercourse, and we're going to help you do it." That's the message a thirteen-year-old receives when he or she is handed a condom. It's an invitation, a statement of expectation, a cheapened view of children. And it's also an erosion of values, caving in on something we know is wrong.

Sex is not for children. People with different values might draw the line in different places, at different ages and circumstances, but a line has to be drawn. And our bottom line is: You can quibble about age, but there is an age at which children should not be having sex. That's where unwanted pregnancies and venereal disease begin, not to mention the negative lessons an adolescent learns about the lack of intimacy, caring, and love. What we should be teaching in our schools, in addition to straightforward medical facts, is "Sex is not for adolescents. Don't do it. You're too young." But instead we propagate the view among thirteen-year-olds that "The officials in school are giving away condoms, so how can having sex be wrong?" Morality is abandoned for the sake of expediency. And, as a result, for many adolescents faced with a difficult choice, sex without responsibility or understanding becomes the rule. And if the people who run our schools are going to be consistent, the next logical step to prevent the spread of AIDS should be giving away needles to thirteen-year-olds.

We believe a positive effort should be made to promote and teach moral values in school. Talk about state-sponsored standards of morality makes many people nervous. They think it smacks of suppression and "Big Brother" images from *1984*. But we're not moving toward "Big Brother" in this country. To the contrary, we're moving in the opposite direction, at times dangerously out of control. Schools are charged with bestowing upon students the knowledge and skills required for a successful life. And we think that should include the promotion of universally recognized values.

Ethics courses in college and graduate school are generally a case of "too little, too late." In reality, they don't encourage right over wrong so much as they teach how to manipulate and justify within the rules. Students attend with a nod and a wink, because by then their values have been substantially formed. The place to begin teaching morals is in kindergarten; perhaps with a discussion of "Jack and the Beanstalk." Was it right for Jack to go into someone else's house without an invitation and steal?

Community service should also be part of the curriculum for grades one through twelve. All students, no matter how deprived, have the ability to help someone else. School programs should enable them to feel connected to the rest of society in a constructive way. "Citizenship" should be graded on report cards. We evaluate how well students perform in history, science, and math. Isn't how they relate to the community-at-large and their peers equally important? And we'd like to see more emphasis in our schools on heroes.

Heroes are important to moral development. They serve as role models and bind people together. Yet, in this day and age, we have celebrities; we have superstars; but we have very few heroes. We took two presidents who were heroes in their own right—Washington and Lincoln—and lumped them together on Presidents' Day, as though the heroic dimension of their lives was in the fact that they were presidents, rather than men of unique foresight, courage, and wisdom. Franklin Roosevelt was a hero, but we don't celebrate his birthday or commemorate his life in any significant way. Martin Luther King, Jr., and John F. Kennedy were wonderful heroes, regardless of what we might know about their sex lives or doctoral theses. Students don't have to believe their heroes are perfect. They can deal with shades of gray. Nor do heroes have to be in political life, or even famous. Local heroes can bind a community, just as national leaders bind a nation. What students do need, though, are role models beyond Mike Tyson and Roseanne, and they should be taught accordingly.

Junior high school and high school students are a particularly good target group for the teaching of moral values. They're old enough to be intellectually curious and to think independently of what their parents have taught them. They have a lot of time to think, and in many respects, their ideas are still unformed. There's a lot they can learn that will make them better citizens if they're taught values by educators who believe in those values and in the students themselves.

Our nation's religious institutions also must rededicate themselves to the task of teaching morals. There's a tendency among congregations today to think that just by showing up at services and going through the rituals of faith, they're fulfilling their commitment to religion. But that type of thinking strikes us as wrong.

We don't believe that religious institutions should make public policy. The folly of that effort has been shown time and time again in American life and in the politics of other countries. But we do think that religious institutions should do more to teach and promote values; to put the Golden Rule back into people's lives, and influence individual conduct on a daily basis.

Also, we believe that organized religion has to move out of its houses of worship and reach out to people, particularly the disadvantaged, in their own environment to make credible the view that it understands these people's lives and cares about them. Too often, religious institutions in this country have ignored the basic needs and problems of the downtrodden. For centuries, slavery was supported by the teaching: "You take your place in the social order. This is your cross to bear. Someday, you will be saved." And even today, among those who have faith, that same message is used to justify all manner of inequity and deprivation. The time has come for religious groups to reach out with renewed effort to identify and help people in need. And a focal point of that effort should be helping parents raise children. That means day care and, where necessary, shelter in houses of worship. It means health care through religious congregations. In some instances, it means things as basic as teaching parents how to enroll their children in school. And it means constantly teaching moral values.

Community programs are also a vehicle by which we can encourage higher moral standards. Aristotle wrote that community is the best teacher of virtue. And there's no doubt that a community can create an environment that leads to shared excellence. We have seen evidence of that in accomplishments ranging from the work of our Founding Fathers to the teamwork of championship football teams. Now, what we have to do within our communities is build a sense of cooperation and develop programs that bring out the best in every individual.

We think of communities most often as geographically defined neighborhoods, although distinctions can be made on the basis of any number of factors. Whatever standard is used, however, communities give their members a sense of identity and belonging. They're extremely important, so much so that, in the absence of constructive community ties, many people—particularly the young—will opt for alternative communities such as cults or gangs.

Our communities need more effective social programs to create an environment in which people are taught decency and have a sense of hope. The Gay Men's Health Crisis and other AIDS support groups have done wonderful, caring work. Inner-city Big Brother and Big Sister programs have brought role models into young people's lives. The key to these programs is individual involvement. Children, in particular, need men and women of character around them; people they can see, talk with, and touch. Someone has to step in and give children a reason to feel good about themselves. Their self-esteem is important, because loving and respecting oneself is a prerequisite to loving and respecting others. People whose greatest accomplishment is simply that they've been married to each other for twenty years and still love each other and are faithful to each other have a great deal to share with children. Many of these couples have never been asked to express themselves or tell anyone what their marriage has meant to them. And they should be encouraged to do so, because they're superb role models. We have to take the time to go after children, bring them into a community setting, and let them know that a good life shared with others is within their grasp.

Television must also be harnessed to improve the moral climate of our nation. We've talked previously about the role television has played in contributing to the erosion of values. But the same factors that allow for negative impact can be utilized in a positive manner.

Television is a relatively young medium; only about forty years old in terms of significant influence. It's the one medium in America that has everyone's attention, particularly that of children. And the power of television is extraordinary. It reflects and shapes values in America, and has the capacity to change the world. Improperly used, it might be dangerous to teach moral values through television. But shows like *Sesame Street* and *Bill Cosby* do just that, with generally positive results. Documentaries such as *Eyes on the Prize*, which traced the civil rights movement in America, perform a service for young and old. When TV movies feature "designated drivers," they remind viewers not to drink and drive. Recent studies of public service advertising campaigns found that television commercials are capable of inducing significant changes in people's behavior regarding health.

The men and women who control television must understand the opportunity to do good at their command. Rather than devote themselves solely to making as much money as possible, it's imperative for them to urge a more critically developed sense of right and wrong within the industry as it relates to what people see and learn from television.

In this day and age, of course, television is inextricably intertwined with politics. And another avenue to instilling better moral values in our society would be more honorable political leadership. The potential of leadership is that it can bring out the best in people. The limits of leadership are that no leader can perform magic. But now, more than ever, we need political leaders who inspire by word and example; leaders with the courage to be guided by what is right, not by what is politically expedient.

Toward that end, we believe that all citizens have a moral obligation to educate themselves regarding the issues involved in political campaigns and to vote. It's very hard to draw a line between the morality of a society and the morality of the individuals who live in it. For example, one might ask, "Can a person live an honorable life, teach his or her children high ethical standards, give money to charity, not break any laws, and at the same time ignore the fact that they live in Nazi Germany; or ignore the institution of slavery; or ignore homeless people sleeping on the streets?"

The answer is that there are many people for whom a public role is not something they're comfortable with, it's a role they don't know how to perform. That's the reason organizations are essential. Charities, environmental groups, and other entities allow individuals who don't have the time, understanding, or wherewithal to deal with larger societal issues to act in accord with their consciences. But rather than promote involvement of this nature, America in recent years has witnessed a contrary phenomenon—one that John Gardner has labeled "the rise of the sophisticated dropout."

"It used to be," writes Gardner, "that those who stood aside from the significant larger concerns of society were mainly people whose perspective had not been broadened by education or people who were too shallow to take any matter seriously. Now we have a whole new category of educated intelligent people who find immensely sophisticated reasons for noncommitment. One means of turning your back on the larger community is to tell yourself that society has fallen into the hands of unworthy people, and that virtuous clear-eyed spirits such as yourself haven't a chance. You can suck that lollipop of self-deceit all your life and die secure in the belief that the world would have been different had they turned it over to you."

Like Gardner, we reject that view. Rather, we

prefer the thoughts of Margaret Mead, who once opined: "Never doubt that a small group of thoughtful committed citizens can change the world. Indeed, it's the only thing that ever has." And toward that end, we'd very much like to see more people involved in building political institutions in a way that puts pressure on the political process. In many respects, traditional political parties don't function properly in this country anymore. Certainly, there's little in the way of party institutions living up to an overriding sense of social responsibility. In the "old days," whatever flaws they had, political parties were able to demand a certain level of competence from would-be officeholders. Now, candidates don't need much at all beyond the ability to get on television and promote themselves as effectively as possible through public relations tutoring in response to polls. People wonder, "How do those charlatans, fakers, and frauds get elected?" They get elected because not enough people are paying attention to the political process, to the political parties and community organizations that form the backbone of government.

The issue of how to get the political process in this country working effectively again given the reality of what it takes to win elections is something of a conundrum. "It will do no good," Walter Lippmann once wrote, "to think poorly of politicians and talk with bated breath about the voters. No more than the kings before them should the people be hedged with divinity, and they are betrayed by the servile hypocrisy which tells them that what is true and what is false and what is right and what is wrong can be determined by their votes." To Lippmann's voice, James Reston has added: "Most of the great political crises of the American past have been resolved not by the zeal and purpose of the people, but by the willpower and obstinacy of their leaders. What is new now is that leaders seem to think that they must follow the nation instead of leading it."

How, then, can we get 260 million Americans of varied views, needs, backgrounds, and political persuasions to address moral issues and other problems through the political process in a way that promotes the public good? The answer to that question, insofar as it resides with politics, depends in significant part on the efforts of one man.

We have a uniquely presidential government. The president of the United States has enormous political power, and in many respects, he is also looked upon as the personification of America's moral values. Whenever the president speaks of a crisis—whether it's the need to draw even with the Soviets in space or to repel the Iraqi invasion of Kuwait—people pay attention if he's serious about the problem. The tone and quality of presidential leadership, for better or for worse, have always impacted on moral values in America. For as Woodrow Wilson once wrote: "The President is the only national voice in affairs. Let him win the admiration and confidence of the country, and no other single force can withstand him. He is the vital place of action in the system."

This country, more than ever, now needs brave, creative leadership in the White House. The president of the United States should be a hero; a symbol of honesty, decency, and fairness. And a president who seizes the initiative and changes the course of this country for the better will leave a legacy of greatness. The opportunity is there for our chief executive if he is willing to seize it. But having said that, we should add that it would be extremely dangerous and self-defeating for Americans to believe that some person on horseback will ride to save us, and all we need do is wait for our leader. For no one leader can solve all our problems. And even if he or she could, new problems would arise. That simply is the nature of living.

What we would like to see, then, both from our leaders and ourselves, is a new beginning. Otherwise, in the very near future, steps outside of the political process as we know it will be required to solve our problems. This new beginning will be dependent upon both personal commitment and institutional action. And if it is to succeed, it will require among other things a commonsense look at morals; an equitable balancing of rights without losing sight of right and wrong.

We have a system of government in our country that promotes individualism, and that is good. We see freedom, entitlements, and human rights as moral issues, and they are. But moral values don't come in small pieces. They're part of an overall societal fabric. And right now in America, we have too many people who are concerned about their own rights and the rights of select groups of individuals, but show very little respect for the rights of society as a whole. They have confused liberty with unrestricted license, and lost sight of the fact that society as a whole is a source of strength for us all.

There will always be tension between the rights of the individual and the rights of society. But in recent years, on too many levels, the balance has swung so far in the direction of the former as to negate social responsibility on the part of many individuals. Someone suffering from contagious tuberculosis who walks the streets can be confined. That's considered a medical issue. But if that same person has AIDS and continues to have sex, it's considered a civil liberties matter, and medical authorities are precluded from notifying his or her sexual partner(s). In many states, a woman who has been raped can't even secure a blood test from her assailant to determine if he has AIDS, except as part of a plea bargain. These extreme interpretations of individual rights fly in the face of decency and logic.

In another area of mounting concern, many recent policy decisions regarding America's homeless population seem to have abandoned common sense in favor of a theory of rights assertible *against* society. Homelessness is a horrible curse, and it's spreading rapidly throughout America. Fifteen years ago, except for scattered enclaves, there were only a handful of homeless people in each urban neighborhood, and many residents knew their names. Now, in many sections of our cities, there are a half-dozen homeless people on every block, and the problem has spread to rural areas as well.

America's homeless need help. They need it for their sake and for ours. For their sake, because each person has only one life to live, and we have to be sensitive to the devastation in other people's lives. The human misery experienced across the American landscape, and particularly in our inner cities, is more than a rhetorical device for politicians or a hustle for people on the dole. It's real. The man or woman sleeping on the street, the crack baby born in despair, is living the only life that he or she will ever have. And each of us must know that relegating them to a lifetime of misery is wrong. And the homeless need help for our sake because pragmatic self-interest, if not moral decency, requires that we help them. "If a free society cannot help the many who are poor," John Kennedy told us in his inaugural address, "it cannot save the few who are rich." And there's a strong argument to be made that unless we do more for America's underclass, particularly the homeless, the entire country will be dragged down.

We need a rebirth of compassion and revitalized social programs to help the homeless. But at the same time, it must be said, being homeless shouldn't absolve people of their responsibility to society or amount to a license to infringe upon the rights of others. Acknowledging the rights of homeless citizens doesn't mean that they should be considered beneath or beyond reasonable standards of accountability. Yet, more and more, that seems to be the path many of our cities are taking.

Thirty years ago, "vagrancy" was a criminal act. There were homeless people in our society, but they were told to stay underground; and if they didn't, they were thrown in jail. Then we moved to the right of people not to be taken off the streets; and after that to the more developed right of every homeless person's entitlement to shelter. But in recent years, the rational balancing test essential to determining rights and obligations has been upset in favor of new standards motivated by misguided compassion that operate to the detriment of society as a whole.

Public amenities exist for the use and enjoyment of all. Parks, libraries, and transportation terminals are among the facilities open to every citizen. They're at the heart of community life. Yet, consider what has happened to these facilities throughout the United States.

Many of our parks have been turned into shantytowns. They're littered with personal belongings and garbage. "Residents" washing up in playground areas render water fountains and toilets unusable. Defenders of this practice voice the refrain, "People should be allowed to live in the parks, because conditions in the homeless shelters are horrible." Yet one wonders what these advocates would say if the shelters were closed as a cost-cutting measure, and homeless people were instructed, "Go live in the park, because conditions there are better than in the shelters anyway."

Our public libraries have become daytime shelters. Often, homeless people come in and sit for hours without reading. Many library users complain that they are stared at endlessly by men and women who are unbathed, smell, spread personal belongings on library tables, and make each trip to the lavatory an exercise in fear. The people hurt most directly by this phenomenon are children who don't have any place safer or better than the library to go to after school.

Our transportation terminals, in many instances, have come to resemble the "black hole of Calcutta." Homeless people lie awake or sleep stretched out on station benches or on the floor. They panhandle, often aggressively, and play loud music. Anyone using a credit card to make a telephone call risks the theft of their credit card number.

When people can no longer enjoy the public parks; when students are afraid to spend an afternoon in the public library; when our transportation terminals are cesspools of petty crime—then we're very much in danger of losing the balance necessary for our society to function properly. Neither of us wants to institutionalize order for its own sake. The suppression of legitimate rights "for the good of society" would be far worse than conditions in America now. But public officials must draw lines between individual rights and public order. Being able to take up residence in the park, loiter in a library lavatory, or panhandle in a bus terminal doesn't improve the quality of a person's life. To the contrary, it detracts from that person's dignity, and diminishes the ability of society to provide amenities for us all. And common sense says that to ignore quality-of-life issues for society at large in favor of antisocial behavior that infringes upon the rights of others is wrong.

We also have some serious commonsense reservations regarding the morality of our current welfare system. Americans try to be fair-minded. When put to the test on public-policy issues, we like to think of ourselves as doing the right thing. Thus, we have constructed an enormous bureaucracy to feed, house, and clothe people without other means. But, in fact, our current welfare programs have become a deterrent to good values.

We believe that a work ethic is essential to good morals. The expression of that ethic can vary. Some people are builders; some are contemplative. We respect diversity, but each of us has a responsibility to be productive and creative, and one of the mechanisms for achieving that is work. We don't see the issue solely in terms of who's on welfare or other forms of public assistance. There are some very rich people in America who don't do much except self-indulgently spend inherited money. They don't act in a productive manner, and we think it's incumbent upon society to separate them from a portion of their wealth so it can be used in a better way. We're in favor of higher taxes when it comes to the nonproductive rich. But we're also in favor of reforming our current system of welfare.

We have no quarrel with welfare when it gives assistance to the elderly or others with no viable alternative. But too often in America today, welfare has been turned into a game. Young, strong, able-bodied people line up for checks, and it makes us mad. And it should make them mad, too, because welfare is a dangerous narcotic. It eliminates work, which is an important part of development, from many people's lives. And it encourages welfare recipients to skirt their obligation to be creative, productive citizens. Also, as a practical matter, we simply can no longer afford to spend increasing billions of dollars each year on stopgap welfare measures that have become a permanent way of life for an ever-increasing segment of our population.

America's welfare programs are in shambles. No one seriously suggests that they're effective anymore, and we'd like to reform them in a fairly simple way. In order to receive public assistance, every person who is physically and mentally able should spend a minimum of four hours a day working in a public service job. The job could be anything the person in question is qualified to do. Reading to blind people, picking up trash on the street, running errands for the elderly, working in a city bus depot. But each person should have to perform community service five days a week to earn their check. Payments for work would be in cash. Other public assistance would take the form of food and clothing. Instead of giving people money for clothes, they'd receive clothing vouchers. Instead of giving people money for food, they'd receive food stamps. And both of these distribution programs should be monitored so the vouchers and stamps aren't misused. These reforms would remove many of the "slackers" from the public assistance rolls. This, in turn, would make more money available for people truly in need. It would lead to more citizens working in ways that would benefit their community, and give them a sense of self-worth as productive members of society.

We also believe that moral values in this country, or at least the climate in which they are generated, can be improved through more effective use of criminal sanctions and other forms of punishment. There are many problems at present in the United States, and one of them is that too many people are breaking the law. We don't think that morality can be dictated. The only road to a truly moral society is to create conditions in which people want to be moral. But there are many people who refrain from committing bad acts because they're afraid of being caught and punished. And if that fear is removed, their conduct degenerates accordingly.

For law enforcement to be effective, people have to feel that swift, certain justice will follow wrongdoing, but that simply isn't the case with our legal system. On average, an estimated 25 million crimes involving violence or significant property loss are committed in the United States each year. Of these, 15 million are reported to the police. There are 3.2 million arrests, 2.6 million criminal prosecutions, 1.9 million convictions, and 500,000 jail sentences. In other words, only 2 percent of all serious crimes committed in the United States each year result in the perpetrator's going to jail.

In the wake of these numbers, judges, legislators, district attorneys, and others campaign for office with the pledge that they will be "tough on crime." Yet, those promises rarely translate into reality, and our courts have become places of accommodation rather than halls of justice. Defendants whittle away at the case against them in pretrial proceedings, at trial, at sentencing, in the appeals process, and in the residual period after parole. The process drags on without adjudication for so long that instead of being "innocent until proven guilty," we have a system that allows some defendants to remain innocent virtually forever. And the same courts that were once symbols of law enforcement are now metaphors for the breakdown of society.

Look at the New York State Supreme Court building in Manhattan. It's a glorious architectur al structure with vaulted ceilings and beautiful murals. Once, it inspired everyone who passed through its doors. Now, the courthouse is filthy and seedy-looking; it smells. People no longer feel safe inside. It's almost degrading to be part of the process that unfolds there each day, whether as a juror, a lawyer, or a party to litigation.

This is not a system that can deal effectively with people who are ripping off America—the drug dealers, the tax cheats, the street muggers, the stock manipulators. Five hundred billion dollars have been lost in the savings and loan scandals, and how many of the people responsible have been indicted, convicted, and sent to jail? From 1987 through 1992, federal bank regulators filed 95,045 criminal referrals with the FBI in connection with the S&L scandal. Seventy-five percent of those referrals were dropped without any criminal prosecution at all, many because of manpower problems. Courts have ordered defendants to pay close to $1 billion in restitution and fines, but less than five percent of that amount has actually been paid. In the end, fewer than five hundred S&L defendants will spend meaningful time in jail, which averages out to more than $1 billion for each defendant subjected to meaningful incarceration. Who says that crime doesn't pay?

We believe that punishment is a deterrent to crime. And we believe that punishment in the form of lengthy prison terms and significant fines where appropriate would be a particularly effective deterrent with regard to white-collar criminals, although many street criminals are equally deserving of lengthy incarceration. We now have a situation in this country whereby serious charges are plea-bargained down to no jail time or thirty days in jail because there aren't enough prosecutors and judges to properly effectuate trials. And even when people are tried and convicted, there often isn't enough room for them in jail. Indeed, the average sentence served for murder in the United States today is six and a half years. We favor spending a lot of money to rectify that situation. People who belong in jail shouldn't be excused from prison because of overcrowding. And they shouldn't draw "community service" either. All community service means in most instances is that the defendant has "beaten the rap."

We know there are limits to what can be accomplished by putting people in prison. Punishment applied arbitrarily or to enforce an unjust system leads only to further inequity and, if oppressive enough, to revolution. At present, in the United States, there are approximately 1.1 million people in federal, state, and local prisons. No other industrialized nation in the world has a higher per capita ratio, and we spend in excess of $20 billion a year on their incarceration. Thus, it's clear that punishment isn't a panacea for what ails America. In the end, it will be necessary for us to eliminate the underlying causes of crime, particularly among the nation's disadvantaged. But there will always be people who belong in prison. And what we should tell them and every other American is: If you want to learn, we'll provide public schools where you can get an education. If you're sick, we'll provide you with medical care that offers the best hope of cure. If you want a job, we'll provide every service possible to help you find one. And if you commit a crime that warrants incarceration, we'll provide you with a prison cell.

We also believe that, apart from the criminal justice system, there should be better self-policing mechanisms with appropriate sanctions among professional groups and other subsections of our society. One of the most disturbing trends in

America today is the reluctance, and in some cases the outright refusal, of people to take steps against wrongdoing by their peers. These "conspiracies of silence" permeate American life, but they're particularly odious when they involve violations of the public trust.

There are certain professions that the public is forced to rely upon in a very special way. When people go to a doctor for treatment, they have no choice but to trust that doctor's integrity and competence. Lawyers are officers of the court, with specialized knowledge unavailable to lay people. They're part and parcel of the legal system, and there's no way courts can handle all of the legal issues that come along without the help of lawyers. Yet doctors perform unnecessary surgery with little fear that their license will be taken away. Lawyers routinely delay litigation, and with varying frequency, wink at perjury, mishandle cases, and otherwise violate the law without sanction. Indeed, several years ago, it was discovered that more than two hundred partners in New York State law firms were failing to file state income tax returns or pay state income taxes in New York. Yet there was no sense of outrage in the legal community; only embarrassment. And in a profession that is supposedly self-regulating, virtually none of the transgressors was disbarred or had their practice of law substantially interrupted.

When men and women refuse to act against misconduct by their peers, it leads to the acceptance of lower moral standards for everyone. We see it among ethnic and religious groups daily. It's common among politicians, police officers, even clergy. Misplaced notions of self-interest and loyalty have eliminated the concept of self-regulation, which once curbed immoral conduct without resort to the criminal law. And as a result, we've moved further than ever from the wisdom of Theodore Roosevelt, who once wrote, "No man is above the law, and no man is below it. Obedience to the law is demanded as a right, not asked as a favor."

Still, punishment and obedience to the law without more are meaningless. And all of the institutional reforms we've suggested must be viewed within the broader framework of "What kind of country do we want to live in? What kind of people do we want to be?"

We've been critical of American society in this book. And, obviously, we feel that criticism is warranted or else we wouldn't have voiced it. But we also believe that this is a great country, and that we as a people should be proud of our heritage. At its worst, America has been ravaged by prejudice, hatred, greed, and violence. But the American spirit has also produced liberty, generosity, great love, and joy. People don't cross the border illegally or risk their lives to travel in small boats from the United States to other countries. But millions of people from around the globe chance everything to come here. And well they might, because in addition to spanning a continent, look at what we've accomplished. We've built a nation with an uninterrupted history of government based on popular consent. We've led the world in technology, served as the "arsenal of democracy" in two world wars, and championed freedom, individual dignity, and human rights. And most of what we've done has been accomplished by a population of immigrants, many of whom were unwanted in their native lands.

Certainly, a nation that has accomplished all that we have achieved is capable of accomplishing more. Our moral climate won't change overnight any more than nature's does. But just as consensus has led to the lowering of moral standards in America, so, too, a broad-based awakening among the American people can raise those standards. The potential for improvement lies within us. And once we've restored our values to their former heights, then we as a nation can seek even higher ground.

Human beings enjoy the most privileged and exalted position in life's creative plan, and we should always strive to justify that honor. Building a more righteous society will be difficult. Prejudice, greed, violence, and hunger are ancient intractable problems. If they were easy to solve, they'd be gone by now. But as Thomas Huxley once wrote: "There is no limit to the extent to which intelligence and will, guided by sound principles and organized in common effort, may modify conditions for a period longer than that now covered by history. And much may be done to change the nature of man himself. The intelligence which has converted the brother of the wolf into the faithful guardian of the flock ought to be able to do something toward curbing the instincts of savagery in civilized men."

Perhaps the best lies ahead. As optimists, we think it does. And if the American people take the lead in seeking a more virtuous spirit, our nation once again will be the envy of the world. But before we change as a nation, we will have to change as individuals.

This book is a strong statement on behalf of community and community values. In the end, though, morals are an individual matter. Even though seeds may be planted by others, values must grow from within. We all come into this world by ourselves, and we will leave it by ourselves. No one enters heaven on a group plan. And for better values to be achieved throughout society, each of us as individuals must do a better job.

How much of a difference can one person make? That's like asking, "What is the value of one life?" In the cosmic scheme of things, the answer might be "Not much." But one can answer with equal validity, "Every life is precious, and every person on Earth matters." We prefer the latter view. We believe that every good person makes the society we live in better and stronger. It all comes down to one person at a time, and that person is you—the reader of this book.

Many people don't understand how good they can be in terms of their own moral core. And that failure to understand our capacity for good goes to the heart of America's moral dilemma. But the beauty of morals is that each individual can control his or her own destiny. In many respects, we're all at the mercy of external forces. Our education, our jobs, our government, our personal relationships—perhaps especially our personal relationships—are dependent in varying degree upon the will of others. But morality is the one area in which every person is endowed with absolute power to be the person he or she wants to be. And once that empowerment is understood, the possibilities for moral development are limitless. Each of us must learn to differentiate between right and wrong, and live our lives accordingly. The search for good values is often hard, but it's an exciting and wondrous voyage of discovery.